TOP LEFT TO BOTTOM RIGHT: *Circa 1812 penny (obverse): a fine representation of the forge at Messrs Cox's iron foundry, Taunton (D Somersetshire 121: 33 mm). 1812 penny (obverse): the ironworks and waterwheel of Messrs I. Bunn and Company at Weybridge Mills (D Surrey 5: 32 mm). 1813 penny (obverse): the mills of the Flint leadworks with a ship alongside a crane (D Flintshire 11: 33 mm). 1811 penny (obverse): the Devon mines at Tavistock (D Devonshire 23: 33 mm).*

TRADE TOKENS OF THE INDUSTRIAL REVOLUTION

Jim Newmark

Shire Publications Ltd

CONTENTS

Set in 10 point Times roman and printed in Great Britain by C. I. Thomas & Sons (Haverfordwest) Ltd, Press Buildings, Merlins Bridge, Haverfordwest.

COVER: *The wide variety of topics depicted on tokens reflected the dominant themes of the times. A few random examples are shown.*

Note. In the captions to the tokens illustrated, the abbreviation DH refers to Dalton and Hamer *Provincial Token-Coinage of the Eighteenth Century*, and D refers to Davis *Nineteenth-Century Token Coinage* (see Further Reading, page 32). The diameter of each token is given at the end of its caption. Except on pages 1 and 2, where only one side of each token is depicted, both sides of the token are shown, with the obverse on the left and the reverse on the right.

LEFT TO RIGHT: *Circa 1795 halfpenny (obverse), illustrating circus riding at the Lyceum, Strand (DH Middlesex 362: 28 mm). 1795 halfpenny (reverse): 'Commerce augments Dundee' (DH Angusshire 10: 27 mm). 1793 halfpenny (reverse): Emsworth shows a flying dove with a cornucopia and 'Peace and plenty' (DH Hampshire 11: 28 mm). 1792 halfpenny (reverse): Donald and Company, stocking manufacturers of Nottingham, emphasise the virtues of busy bees (DH Nottinghamshire 8: 28 mm).*

LEFT TO RIGHT: *1794 halfpenny (reverse): 'For change not fraud' (DH Herefordshire 5: 28 mm). 1796 halfpenny (obverse): 'Success to the port of Leith' (DH Lothian 58: 28 mm). 1797 farthing (obverse): the horse and cart with bales from the Dundee flax hackling works (DH Angusshire 42: 22 mm). 1814 halfpenny (reverse): issued by R. Romanis of Cheapside, London, showing a stocking frame of the type designed in the sixteenth century (D Middlesex 62: 28 mm).*

TOP: *1795 halfpenny. John Skidmore manufactured these fine register stove grates at his iron foundry in Clerkenwell, London. He was stove grate maker to HM Board of Ordnance. (DH Middlesex 480: 28 mm.)*
BOTTOM: *1797 halfpenny. A fine example of the work of the designer James Wright junior. (DH Perth 2: 26 mm.)*

INTRODUCTION

Looking at tokens we can directly sense the spirit of the age in which they appeared. They provide contact with the thoughts and desires of past generations. The period of the industrial revolution is especially rich in documentation presented by tokens. They reveal to us an astonishing panorama of the life of a people undergoing profound changes never before experienced in the history of Britain.

From an understanding and study of tokens we can get a deeper appreciation of the problems affecting our forbears. They were responding to the ineptitude and inefficiency of their rulers in ignoring a basic necessity for their daily existence. This was the provision of sufficient small coinage at a time when even a farthing was of real value.

How they overcame for a time official inertia and provided their own solution to a pressing problem will be outlined in the following pages. The outpouring of popular feeling expressed in the inscriptions on tokens was on a scale unparalleled in former times.

The official regal coinage had never reflected contemporary events. The tokens of the late eighteenth and early nineteenth centuries took full advantage of their unofficial issue to make good this deficiency.

To obtain a fair perspective of the historical necessity for the appearance of tokens it is important to look back to their early origins. It is a fascinating story of popular initiative against the disdain and misrule of established authority.

EARLY TOKENS

The frequent appearance of tokens throughout history was due to the lack of sufficient small coinage for the people's daily needs. This was evident as far back as 1300 in the reign of Edward I. He then issued leathern money to spare more valuable silver bullion. This was used by tradesmen to pay the wages of workmen engaged in the building of Caernarvon and other Welsh castles. In 1404 the House of Commons was 'petitioning the King to help solve the lack of small coinage by issuing lead tokens'. Also, it is recorded that during the reign of Henry VIII (1509-47) 'private tokens were used to supply the want of silver coins'.

Later, at the time of Elizabeth I (1558-1603) 'the use of private tokens for money, which was stamped by inferior tradesmen, was at this time grown to such an excess as to be the subject of frequent complaints'. Also, 'they were made of Lead, Tin, Latten, and even of Leather. Of these base materials were found Farthings and Halfpence, to the great derogation of the princely honour and dignity, and the great loss of the poor, since they were only to be repaid to the shop from whence they were first received.'

Rising discontent against the continued shortage of small change was becoming evident in the reign of James I (1603-25). The smallest coin in circulation was the fine silver halfpenny, awkward to handle in everyday use and of too high a value for ordinary retail transactions. The monarch's response to these tribulations was to award in 1613 a lucrative monopoly to his favourite, Lord Harrington, to issue 'a competent quantity of Farthing Tokens of Copper'.

Both the King and the noble lord made considerable profits from this transaction; £25,000 was the sum estimated to have been netted by Lord Harrington alone. The farthings he issued were, however, so tiny (some weighing only 3 grams, or a tenth of an ounce) and so easily counterfeited, and thus a prey to widespread forgeries, that they sorely tried the patience of tradesmen.

The discontent of the people was not allayed by this ineffective measure; some years later, in 1648, people took matters in their own hands and began to produce their own first, widespread issue of token coinage.

SEVENTEENTH-CENTURY TOKENS

The initiative came from individual traders who stamped the tokens with their names and trades and their wives' initials, also dates and devices. Very soon followed the tokens issued by local government bodies, overseers of the poor, churchwardens and other officials. These were mainly of farthing value; it is estimated that over twelve thousand types of token were issued in Great Britain, 3,500 in London alone.

Their inscriptions seem quaint to us today, but they provide valuable records for local historians. Large numbers of these strange, interesting coins have survived. They are a link with the past, with the merchants, innkeepers, market traders and the commercial life of the times.

Their popularity is evident by the wide circulation that they enjoyed. They gave much needed relief to the sorely tried population, victims of continual neglect by the authorities. Coins of base metal, considered by Queen Elizabeth I to be unsuitable as regal currency and demeaning to royal dignity, had become acceptable as an everyday means of exchange.

The abuses that followed from their unofficial and unregulated issue led to growing complaints and petitions. Forging and underweight tokens undermined confidence in their use, and by 1672 it was decided by the Privy Council to stamp out these malpractices. An official issue of regal copper farthings and halfpence of superior weight and design effectively replaced for a while the circulation of token coinage. Further problems, however, arose in connection with the maldistribution of the new copper coins. The authorities were not much nearer to solving the problem of providing sufficient small change for daily use.

T. S. Ashton, the noted economic historian, asserts that 'the supply of legal money was far from adequate to the needs of an expanding economy and much inconvenience and social disharmony arose from a shortage of coins suitable for the payment of wages for retail transactions. For this state of affairs part of the responsibility lay with the Royal Mint, a body which, though answerable to the Treasury, preserved many of the features of the privileged corporations of Stuart times.'

The Master of the Mint, even up to 1799, received his remuneration from a commission on output. It was more profitable to him to produce gold rather than silver coins, in larger rather than smaller denominations. The Mint had no distribution system of its own and heavy costs were entailed in moving bulky coinage to distant parts of the country. The country banks, small in number in the mid eighteenth century, but growing to over three hundred by 1799, had few facilities for handling the copper change increasingly in demand.

Apart from the neglect of the common need for sufficient small change a further burden was the widespread practice of truck payments. Many contemporary accounts expose the abuses suffered. One report notes 'the system which we see in the Duke of Bridgewater's colliery village near Manchester, where wages were paid monthly, and the collier merely received in cash the surplus after the shopkeeper's bills had been paid'.

The Duke was the builder of the first of the English canals, cut from Worsley to Manchester. An entry from his book of accounts in 1771 shows payment of £35 14s 6½d to Edward Topping and thirty-two more labourers for a month's wages for cutting the canal at Runcorn. The average was just over five shillings a week; the money was paid periodically in a lump sum to the leader of the gang.

Samuel Oldknow, the Anderton spinner, made extensive use of the truck system by paying his workers with bills . . . 'the workers disliked this system, for they had to pay 3d per £1 to the local shopkeeper for cashing.' John Wilkinson, the famed ironmaster and issuer of his own tokens, paid his workers at Bersham foundry and at his coal and lead mines every Saturday with assignats. These were the depreciated French currency brought over to England.

Manchester linen drapers and Rochdale clothiers who provided raw materials and yarn to country manufacturers had to make payments in cloth due to shortage of currency. Also, Sheffield factors paid the small masters for their cutlery and files in steel and other commodities.

These abuses arose from the dearth of coinage, but the pernicious practices of the truck system did not end when currency was more plentiful; it continued far into the nineteenth century.

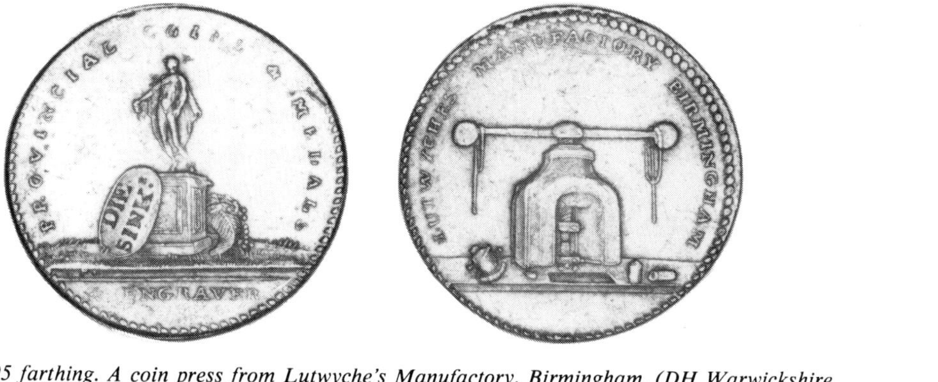

Circa 1795 farthing. A coin press from Lutwyche's Manufactory, Birmingham. (DH Warwickshire 482: 22 mm.)

1787 penny. The premier token of the eighteenth century. (DH Anglesey 17-85: 33 mm.)

EIGHTEENTH-CENTURY TOKENS

The gathering pace of the industrial revolution brought increasing need for greater amounts of currency. More and more workers were being employed in the new manufacturing enterprises. Mining was being extensively undertaken, often in isolated areas by newly formed companies. These ventures into new fields, in conjunction with the rapid growth of urban communities, meant the need for payments of large amounts of money wages to the new proletariat.

The time was opportune for a great new upsurge in the supply of tokens to offset the chronic dearth of official coinage. The first large issuer was Thomas Williams, an industrial magnate, owning copper mines in Anglesey, smelting works in other areas, and also coining presses in Birmingham. He began in 1787 to produce his own tokens. They were finely designed and of full weight; over 300 tons — about thirty million tokens — were made. The classical, traditional emblem of a Druid was engraved, together with the cypher *PMCo* (Parys Mines Company) on the reverse.

These were the earliest large-scale issue of the late eighteenth century. Unfortunately, they bore no representations of the processes of industry; they show no location of their places of work. Later issues of other tokens were to reveal fascinating glimpses of the growing industrial technology and to express feelings aroused by the profound changes ushered in by the new age.

Another major industrialist, John Wilkinson, also in 1787, began to issue his famous series of tokens with his head stamped upon them. He liked to be known as the 'king of the iron world' and had no qualms about its obvious similarity to the King's portrait.

Wilkinson was a leading ironmaster with works in various places in Shropshire, Staffordshire and Clwyd. Among his achievements were a new method of boring cylinders, the production of iron pipes, assisting in the building of the first iron bridge at Coalbrookdale, and constructing the first iron ship. Matthew Boulton and James Watt were close associates from whom he obtained cylinders and other iron parts for steam engines.

Charles Roe of Macclesfield also issued a large number of tokens bearing his portrait and on the reverse a figure holding a drill with a worm and cogwheel. He started as a silk manufacturer and later acquired copper mines in Anglesey. His memorial tablet in Christ Church, Macclesfield, has a lengthy inscription detailing his achievements.

The genuine 'trade tokens' issued by

these major companies were acceptable over a wide area and the edge readings (writing round the rims) showed where they could be redeemed in coins of the realm. They were of full weight, well made, and enjoyed the confidence of large numbers of people. Other tokens, however, issued by lesser known manufacturers and traders, were mainly restricted in circulation to their own localities.

Traders, whose business took them to many parts of Britain, were often faced with the problems of convertibility. The shopkeepers used sorting boxes to store the assortment of tokens, arranging them by the names of issuers in the locality. Bankers did not relish the task of transferring consignments of copper tokens to their places of origin for redemption.

The very success and acceptability of the tokens attracted, as previously, the counterfeiters and forgers. There was the inducement of considerable profit from making fraudulent coins. These were more crudely produced and lighter in weight. Often they bore no issuer's name and address. Shopkeepers anxious to push their wares offered tokens, which were a valuable means of advertising. These were inscribed with their name, address and business, and acceptable in a limited area.

The fashion of collecting tokens began to spread, inducing token manufacturers to issue pieces often of superior workmanship and design. These series include those issued by Kempson, illustrating historical buildings and forming valuable records of architectural interest. It is worth noting the sentiments expressed on many of these non-currency tokens. They were part of the general thinking of the time.

It is estimated that over ten thousand different types of token made their appearance during the period from 1787 to 1817. The issuers comprised a wide range of commercial enterprises, including merchants, shopkeepers, transport undertakings, publishers, workhouse masters and political factions. Tokens gave vent to the widest expression of popular opinion. Looking at their inscriptions today, one can sense the deep feelings engendered in the people by the onset of a troubled, uncertain age. At least a partial relief was offered by the appearance of the tokens, as contemporary accounts in periodicals amply testify.

Manufacturers and issuers of tokens were quick to exploit popular feeling; they offered appropriate sentiments in keeping with their wares. The profits they made were substantial but they provided an essential service to the community.

F. D. Klingender, in an article written in 1943, makes a telling comment: 'tokens had become a superb medium not only for commercial advertisement, but also for every other type of propaganda, and that at a time when the minds of men were teeming with new ideas in science, technology and economics, when their hearts responded to the appeals of the philanthropists and when

1790 halfpenny. Portrait of John Wilkinson. The reverse shows the interior of a smithy with a workman placing a piece of metal under a large drop hammer. (DH Warwickshire 388: 28 mm.)

1794 halfpenny. Canterbury Cathedral. Reverse: the arms of the city. (DH Kent 7: 28 mm.)

their passions were inflamed by the challenge of the French Revolution. In reflecting all these interests and aspirations, the tokens are a matchless record, not of the opinions of fashionable society in the metropolis, but of the outlook of the people at large in all parts of the country.'

SOCIAL AND POLITICAL TOKENS

We can observe this free expression of opinion on the tokens issued by the shopkeepers and merchants throughout Britain. Of their wide diversity only a small selection can be noted here. From Canterbury, a plea is made for *Unity, peace and concord and goodwill to all men.* A London trader, Robert Orchard, inscribes *Liberty, peace, commerce.* From Norwich come the cries of *Good times will come* and *Peace and plenty* (a response to the Napoleonic wars). Also from Norwich is a token with *Prosperity to old England* on one side and *More trade and fewer taxes* on the other. Other plaintive and common sentiments expressed are: *For the public good; A snail may put his horns out; May a flowing trade follow a speedy and honourable peace; For change not fraud.* The last is a common plea for redress against the circulation of fraudulent, worthless tokens. *Nothing without industry* and *Industry leads to honour* are precepts appropriate for the expanding economy. Lancashire proclaims *Unanimity is the strength of society.* A London token shows a stag with the wording *Freedom with innocence* — a harking back to pre-industrial days.

It is the political tokens, however, that reveal the deep questioning and agitation affecting people in an age of rapid change. Their worn condition, evident in the numbers existing today, indicates their wide circulation. The great public interest aroused in the trials of the famous radicals Thomas Hardy, Hon. T. Erskine, Tooke, Gibbs and others are expressed in many tokens. The London Corresponding Society illustrates the fable of the bundle of sticks and proclaims *United for a reform of Parliament.* Joseph Priestley, the scientist, is hailed *Citizen of the world,* and on the reverse side is shown the tomb of *Hampden and Sidney,* from which the flame of liberty appears.

The greatest political propagandist of the period was Thomas Spence (1750-1814). His tokens contain the most outspoken and hard hitting expressions of opinion that illuminated current thinking. He was a single-minded utopian, believing in his 'glorious plan' and 'partnership in land without private landlordism', which would 'produce everlasting peace and happiness, or in fact, the millennium'.

Many regarded him as a crank, but he had a genius for vivid, popular imagery, which, displayed on his numerous tokens, attracted wide attention. He was a poor schoolmaster from Newcastle and, coming to London in 1792, soon was in the thick of the political turmoil of the day. He was promptly arrested for selling the banned publication of Paine's *Rights of Man.* The following year he was again arrested, twice acquitted, three times indicted and imprisoned for seven months without trial.

Setting up as a token dealer, he sold genuine tokens as well as those of his own manufacture. Most of them were designed by the engraver Charles James; Spence's

Circa 1794 halfpenny. R. Dinmore of Norwich, general merchant, shows a bottle to draw attention to his wares, together with expressing forceful sentiments. (DH Norfolk 24: 29 mm.)

Circa 1794 halfpenny. The trial of the Honourable T. Erskine. (DH Middlesex 1010: 28 mm.)

1795 halfpenny. London Corresponding Society — a dove of peace. (DH Middlesex 286: 29 mm.)

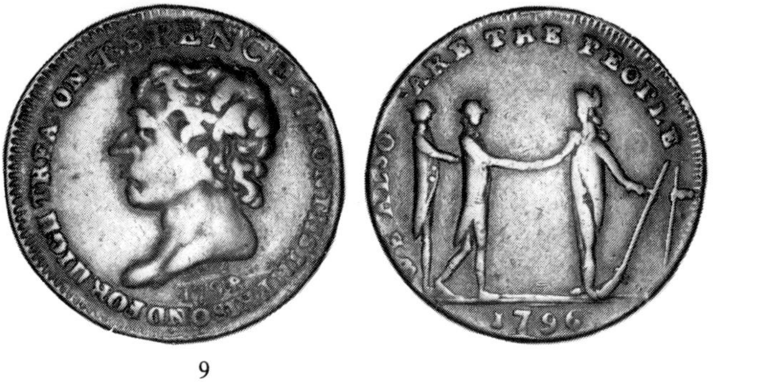

1796 halfpenny. Bust of Thomas Spence. Reverse: 'We also are the people'. (DH Middlesex 691: 28 mm.)

Circa 1794 halfpenny. Spence: the burdened ass and 'After the revolution'. (DH Middlesex 722: 28 mm.)

Circa 1794 farthing. Spence: Adam and Eve, 'Man over man he made not lord'. (DH Middlesex 1088: 20 mm.)

Circa 1794 farthing. Spence: 'Am I not thine ass'. (DH Middlesex 1085: 21 mm.)

1794 halfpenny. Spence: pig's meat. (DH Middlesex 842: 27 mm.)

1794 halfpenny. Recalling a lost freedom. (DH Bedfordshire 3: 29 mm.)

1794 halfpenny. Appledore windmill. (DH Kent 3: 29 mm.)

friend Thomas Bewick also lent valuable assistance. About sixty-eight different dies are known to have been used; their combinations form hundreds of varieties. Some examples mentioned here will illustrate his striking slogans. His own favourite showed the cat; it could be stroked down, but not against the grain.

A token depicts the cat with the wording *My freedom I among slaves enjoy 1796*. The other side has his portrait inscribed *T. Spence. 7 months imprison'd for high treason.* Another has a caricature of a man handcuffed and in irons, with his mouth padlocked, worded *A free born Briton.* This is a telling commentary on the passing of the Libels (or Gagging) Act in 1795. A token shows an ass weighed down with two panniers labelled *Rent* and *Taxes. I was an ass to bear the first pair.* In another a pig is trampling on the emblems of royalty. The wording states *Pig's meat published by T. Spence London. Pig's Meat or Lessons for the Swinish Multitude* was a penny weekly published by Spence between 1793 and 1795; its title was a reference to Burke's notorious phrase 'the swinish multitude'.

A farthing token recalls the idyllic days of Adam and Eve in the Garden of Eden. *Man over man he made not lord* is proclaimed. Other political tokens feature Pitt, Fox and the anti-Paine faction. None of them so memorably record the stormy passions aroused at the time as those issued by Spence.

INDUSTRY

The growing fascination with the new industrial techniques is amply recorded on many tokens. A number, however, reveal wistful glances back to a happier, pre-industrial age. Then people were not herded into what Blake described as 'dark, Satanic mills'. A token from Leighton Buzzard depicts a girl working lace in the open under a shady tree. Another, from Appledore in Kent, shows a man carrying a sack of corn to a windmill; on the other side a lion and a lamb are lying together; the inscription is *Peace innocence and plenty.*

Many tokens display the time-honoured

1796 halfpenny. Spinning at a wheel. 'Sail canvas manufactory'. Reverse: handloom weaving. (DH Devon 6: 28 mm.)

1794 halfpenny. Weaver at loom. Reverse: 'Pro bono publico'. Cipher IF, the initials of the issuer, John Fincham. (DH Suffolk 31: 28 mm.)

handloom, to be seen at Rochdale, Plymouth, Norwich, Haverhill and other centres. They offer pride in a craft that was to be the victim of the new, power-driven machines. The process of flax heckling at Dundee and a girl with a watering can bleaching cloth at Perth are other examples of pre-industrial practices.

The early issues of large quantities of tokens by the Anglesey Mines, Wilkinson and Charles Roe have been mentioned previously. Other enterprises proudly display their workplaces, many showing the products manufactured. A finely designed token of the Carmarthen Ironworks is by Hancock, who also engraved the Wilkinson series. It is of remarkable detail and power, illustrating the interior of the spacious works. The minutely drawn brickwork and heavy roof beams are clearly visible; the men are shown working at the new processes of ironmaking.

Another splendid example of contemporary industrial innovation is seen in the token of the Dublin Rolling Mills. There two men are feeding a strip of iron between rollers, with a flywheel in the background. The Withymoore Scythe Works in Staffordshire has two fine tokens showing the forge shop with the beam engine, probably one of Watt's rotative engines. A huge tilt hammer welds and shapes a bar of iron held by a workman. Today, one can see a reconstruction of the workshop and the identical machinery at the Abbeydale Industrial Hamlet, South Sheffield. The Soho Manufactory of Boulton and Watt and their new brassworks are shown on two tokens in the style of fine country houses. Many of the great manufacturers had their factories designed to emulate the mansions of the gentry. Here the buildings are set in fine parkland by a millpool, disguised as an ornamental lake. The confident Boulton, when visited by Boswell in 1776, said to him, 'I sell here what all the world desires, power.'

A Birmingham token was issued by James Bisset, an enterprising Scot and author of *A Poetic Survey around Birmingham,* published in 1800. In it he extols Soho: 'there stands Soho!

Soho! where Genius and the Arts preside,
Europe's wonder and Britannia's pride.'

1797 halfpenny. Dudhope Castle. Reverse: a man working flax, with details of flax and hemp imports in Dundee. (DH Angusshire 18: 28 mm.)

1792 halfpenny. The ironworks of John Morgan. One of the finest tokens illustrating the new processes of the industrial revolution. (DH Carmarthenshire 7: 29 mm.)

1813 penny. Interior of the Dublin rolling mills. (D Dublin 11: 34 mm.)

Circa 1794 halfpenny. Bisset's Museum and classical temple. (DH Warwickshire 120: 29 mm.)

He portrays on his token obelisks and neo-classical vases to advertise his museum of antiquities.

Another fine representation of factory building is the Albion Mills, built by Rennie and Watt in 1787, bringing the industrial revolution into the heart of London. It contained fifty millstones set in motion by two large engines. Soon it became a favourite visiting place of society; Watt in expressing his annoyance to Boulton wrote: 'What have Dukes, Lords and Ladies to do with masquerading in a flour mill?'

The famed Iron Bridge at Coalbrookdale is justly celebrated, with the remarkable inclined plane of the Ketley Canal shown on the reverse. This important record depicts one of the finest achievements of the early industrial age. At the Ironbridge Gorge Museum today one can witness the pioneering work of Abraham Darby and his colleagues in that extraordinary inventive period.

No less remarkable as an engineering feat was the construction of the iron bridge at Sunderland. This was completed in 1796 at a cost of £40,000. Some of the materials used were taken from a bridge designed by Tom Paine for the Schuykill river in Philadelphia. The span of the Sunderland bridge was 236 feet (72 m) and the height 100 feet (30 m); 260 tons of iron were used in its construction. This magnificent work so captured the public imagination that large numbers of commemorative jugs, bowls and mugs were produced with transfers of the bridge. It was a fashion started at Coalbrookdale; this has persisted even to recent times to celebrate prominent public personages and events.

Klingender points out that these two bridges were the first manifestations of the industrial revolution to impress themselves on the popular artists of the day. The most important were Joseph Wright of Derby, Paul Sandby and William Beilby, among many others who recorded the scenes and wonders around them. The best and most illuminating study of this subject is Klingender's *Art and the Industrial Revolution.*

TRANSPORT

The canals, turnpike roads and later railways played a vital part in the development and growth of economic life. The few tokens that record this, however, are of much interest. The illiterate James Brindley built the first canal (1761-7) for the Duke of Bridgewater between Worsley and Manchester. A token shows a porter carrying a sack of cotton on his back with the wording *Success to navigation.* Other canal tokens feature the Gloucester and Berkeley Canal, the Thames and Severn Canal, and the Stort Navigation. These present the impressive architectural and construction works of the canal pioneers.

Road transport is illustrated in John Palmer's Mail Coach token, in Ibberson's, proclaiming *Mail and post coaches to all parts of England,* and in that of W. Wilson, proprietor of the Swan with Two Necks, Lad Lane, London, offering *Speed, regularity and security.* A rare turnpike token of Walcot, near Bath, is a reminder of the trust monopolies that were empowered to levy tolls for maintaining their stretch of road.

TRADESMEN

The wide variety of tokens issued by shopkeepers and small tradesmen illustrates the thriving commercial activities carried on. They are the earliest examples of persuasive advertising techniques, used together with the dominant sentiments of the time. Booksellers, curriers, saddlers, umbrella makers, hatmakers, candle moulders, sellers of oil for lamps, proprietors of circuses for entertainment and provision merchants are among the most expressive advocates of their offerings. The bookseller Lackington, of Finsbury Square, London, proclaims himself the *Cheapest bookseller in the world.* His extensive stock comprised over a hundred thousand volumes, and his premises were known as the 'Temple of the Muses'. Lackington had seven tons (about seven hundred thousand) of his tokens struck, the largest number issued by any London tradesman.

A harnessmaker, Kelly of the Strand, features a saddled horse, with riding accoutrements on the reverse. Also shown is an umbrella, recently introduced into England by Jonas Hanway after visiting Persia in the mid eighteenth century. This received a mixed reception, for it posed a threat to the livelihood of hackney coachmen and sedan carriers. Rain brought them increased business; with the

1792 halfpenny. Coalbrookdale, the first iron bridge. (DH Shropshire 16: 29 mm.)

1793 halfpenny. Issued by J. Fielding, grocer of Manchester. (DH Lancashire 135a: 28 mm.)

1795 halfpenny. Brimscombe Port. A barge with striped sails. Reverse: the fine architectural entrance to a tunnel. (DH Gloucestershire 60: 28 mm.)

1794 halfpenny. Lackington the bookseller has a figure of Fame, blowing a trumpet. (DH Middlesex 353: 28 mm.)

Circa 1795 halfpenny. A fine display by Kelly of the Strand. He offers harness, saddles and accoutrements. (DH Middlesex 345: 27 mm.)

1795 halfpenny. The Baker's Halfpenny token. (DH Middlesex 297: 28 mm.)

aid of umbrellas people braved the elements.

Another token has reference to social conditions. This was the Baker's Halfpenny issued in 1795. It is inscribed *To lessen the slavery of Sunday baking and provide for public wants: an Act was passed AD 1794*. This measure gave some relief and helped prevent many of the abuses prevalent in that trade.

Many tokens honour the memory of John Howard FRS, the slave trade reformer. One issued from Portsmouth displays its coat of arms and a portrait of Howard. He devoted his life to the study of conditions in prisons at home and abroad. His influential work, *The State of Prisons in England and Wales,* was published in 1777. Portsmouth honoured him for his efforts to alleviate the lot of the inmates of the prison hulks in Portsmouth harbour; it was reported that one third of the prisoners died before the time for their release.

Another token from Bath features John Howard; on the reverse it exhorts viewers to *Remember the debtors in gaol.* This shows a benevolent figure directing a boy with a huge key to open the prison gates. The message draws attention to the common practice of incarcerating people who could not meet small debts. Having no means of paying, they often remained in prison for life. Benevolent societies were formed to relieve their distress and help secure their release.

The spectacle of a chained negro slave is featured on one token; the kneeling and supplicating figure of the slave was first designed for Josiah Wedgwood in 1786 and used for a cameo sold as a campaign badge in thousands on behalf of the Society for the Suppression of the Slave Trade.

The hazards associated with the securing of essential oil supplies are illustrated in a graphic token issued by John Fowler, oil merchant of Long Acre, London. He shows a crew in a whaling boat about to harpoon a whale. This was a highly risky operation; the sympathy of the public was invited for these brave men. Now we have more sympathy for the whale.

Many other instances of forceful and clever advertising techniques can be found on the numerous tokens proliferating all

1794 halfpenny, Portsmouth honours the memory of John Howard. (DH Hampshire 54: 28 mm.)

Circa 1794 halfpenny. Kneeling slave in chains. 'Am I not a man and a brother.' (DH Middlesex 1038: 28 mm.)

1794 halfpenny. The Bath token of M. Lambe and Son, tea dealers and grocers. (DH Somersetshire 50K: 29 mm.)

1795 halfpenny. A two-headed cow and a toucan displayed by Pidcock — part of his numerous collection. (DH Middlesex 454: 28 mm.)

over Britain. A grocer from Bath points the connection between his *Teas coffee spices & sugars* and a laden camel with the rays of a blazing sun overhead. The reverse depicts the frontage of *India House 1794*. Shoes, hats and gloves, glasses and tea sets, stoves and grates are among the articles of commerce displayed on tokens; they are linked to appealing inscriptions. An insight into the popular entertainment of the times is provided by the tokens of Pidcock. He owned the Menagerie at Exeter Change, Strand, where he exhibited a large number of animals and birds. His circuses toured throughout Britain to the wonderment of local people. Boulter's Exhibition of Natural and Artificial Curiosities recorded on a Yarmouth token is another example of a display attracting public interest.

The issue of late eighteenth-century tokens, acceptable to the people at large, was soon coming to an end. The rising price of copper, resulting from a threat of war in 1792, led to the melting down of full-weight tokens and coin. Also the craze for special issues of collectors' tokens and the depredations of counterfeiters caused increasing public anxiety about the real worth of tokens.

The deteriorating situation made the Treasury at last determine to take action; in 1797 a huge contract was awarded to Matthew Boulton to produce at his Birmingham Soho Mint over 1,000 tons of copper coinage. This alleviated the shortage for a time, but the continuing rise in the price of copper resulted in further melting down of these famous 'cartwheels'. No further tokens appeared until a few years later in 1804.

NINETEENTH-CENTURY TOKENS

A much increased labour force needed larger amounts of copper coinage. Shortages throughout Britain again brought forward demands for tokens. By 1811 a flood of new issues began to appear, mainly from prominent manufacturers. The largest of these issuers was Samuel Fereday, 'the greatest ironmaster in the world', employing nearly five thousand people. He issued over two million tokens. Most were of penny denomination, reflecting rising prices under wartime inflation. Silver tokens were also issued during this period; they appeared to be more useful for paying wages than for daily purchases. They offer little of interest in their inscriptions; their utilitarian nature is a shadow of the fresh, vivid designs of the previous century's copper issues.

The new wave of nineteenth-century tokens gives further evidence of the advances in industrial development. Fereday's extensive ironworks and collieries are displayed on many of his tokens. The Sedbury Ironworks has a view of the mill with four chimneys emitting smoke.

The Phoenix Ironworks at Sheffield shows cannon and cannonballs in front of the large building. Roscoe Place displays its range of mills with fourteen chimneys — an early record of one of the huge workplaces for the new proletariat. One of the more picturesque tokens is that issued at Scorrier House, Redruth, Cornwall. It illustrates the three staple products of the county—fish, tin and copper. On the reverse is shown a mine engine house with the beam of a Newcomen pumping engine and a whim or horse-powered winding machine. Many other tokens offer documentary evidence of the accelerating pace of the industrial revolution.

WORKHOUSES

Also appearing are the series of tokens issued by the workhouse authorities. They are a reminder of the degrading and inhuman conditions suffered by a large section of the population. The 1722 Act encouraged the building of workhouses; anyone refusing to enter this last refuge forfeited all claim to relief. The greater part of the working classes depended upon poor relief in old age. In 1793 the Essex hamlet of Thaxted had thirty-nine burials — and thirty of these were of paupers.

The fortress-like structures that housed

Circa 1812 penny. The Sedbury Iron Works. (D Gloucestershire 16: 33 mm.)

1813 penny. Sheffield: the Phoenix ironworks — an early display of armaments. (D Yorkshire 139: 34 mm.)

1812 penny. Sheffield: the Roscoe Mills with smoking chimneys. (D Yorkshire 141: 33 mm.)

1811 penny. Issued by the mine owner John Williams of Scorrier House. (D Cornwall 19-24: 34 mm.)

the inmates of the workhouses are depicted on some of the tokens. Birmingham, one of the earliest issuers in 1796, shows its forbidding exterior erected in 1733. The left wing contained the infirmary; the right wing housed the workshops. There the manufacture of pack thread and the spinning of mop yarn were carried on.

Sir Francis Eden, in his extensive reports *The State of the Poor, 1797,* records the activities of the inmates engaged in the manufacture of various articles of general use; these include shirt and glove making, knitting stockings, packing hair, carding wool, flax spinning, making clothing and bedding. In the absence of regal coinage tokens were used as payments for these tasks, providing the currency for the purchase of provisions and other necessities.

Sheffield workhouse authority issued its token with a figure of Justice; her eyes are bandaged and she carries an olive branch and a pair of scales. The grim exterior is shown on the obverse side. Tunstead in Norfolk, still existing a century later, has a symbol of a wheatsheaf to indicate its links with the agriculture of the district. Keighley and Bradford both used countermarked tokens as a measure of economy. They overstamped with their own imprint the genuine circulating issues of lead and copper companies. Keighley Overseers of the Poor used their penny tokens to pay their paupers in 1818. Bradford later supplanted its workhouse by a new building in 1852 at a cost of £40,000.

When the final Act of Suppression of 1817 forbad the manufacture of further tokens, the workhouse issues were exempted for a few more years. It was recognised that distress and hardship would result from their withdrawal. The bulk of people, however, holding worthless, unredeemable tokens, were the main sufferers.

The end of official tolerance of token circulation came when their depreciated value could no longer be endured by the long suffering public. The unchecked abuses of coiners and counterfeiters, the continual rise in the price of copper and the banking crisis of 1816 brought insistent demands for the authorities to act. They were finally compelled to do so; the Act of 1817 could not absolve them, however, for the long neglect of their public responsibilities. The tokens remain as an imperishable record of popular initiative and response during those eventful times.

1812 penny. Birmingham Workhouse. The reverse states 'One pound note payable at the workhouse for 240 tokens'. (D Warwickshire 37-41: 36 mm.)

1813 penny. Sheffield Workhouse. (D Yorkshire 126-33: 33 mm.)

1812 penny. Tunstead and Happing Workhouse token. (D Norfolk 29: 34 mm.)

1818 penny. Countermarked Keighley Workhouse token. (Yorkshire CM 51: 35 mm.)

1818 penny. Countermarked Bradford Workhouse token. (Yorkshire CM 50: 34 mm.)

Ancient Colchester Castle. Reverse: handloom; 'Success to the bay trade'. Baize and serge (bay) manufacture was a staple trade.

1792 halfpenny. Arms and crest of Rochdale. Reverse: weaving at a loom. (DH Lancashire 144: 29 mm.)

1793 halfpenny. Shrewsbury shield of arms. Reverse: woolsack — 'Salop woollen manufactory.' (DH Shropshire 19-22: 29 mm.)

Circa 1812 penny. A weaver working at a loom. Issued by Jackson and Listers, linen manufacturers and bleachers of Barnsley. (D Yorkshire 75-8: 33 mm.)

1795 halfpenny. Issued by J. Moore, linen draper of Great Portland Street, London. (DH Middlesex 389: 28 mm.)

1794 halfpenny. 'Success to trade and commerce'. Token from Braintree, an important market town. (DH Essex 4: 28 mm.)

1796 halfpenny. Tenterden brewery shows a dray and horse with the apt inscription 'To cheer our hearts'. (DH Kent 42: 28 mm.)

1793 halfpenny. The legend of Lady Godiva riding through Coventry. (DH Warwickshire 242: 27 mm.)

1792 halfpenny. Dr Samuel Johnson honoured on a Birmingham token. (DH Warwickshire 71a: 28 mm.)

1795 halfpenny. Emsworth commemorates Earl Howe and 'The wooden walls of old England'. (DH Hampshire 30: 27 mm.)

1793 halfpenny. Sir Isaac Newton. (DH Middlesex 1034: 27 mm.)

1791 halfpenny. Remembering Handel's charitable work. (DH Middlesex 1022: 27 mm.)

1793 halfpenny. Bishop Blaize, patron saint of woolcombers. Reverse: the fine Leeds Cloth Hall. (DH Yorkshire 29-41: 28 mm.)

1795 halfpenny. Thomas Haycraft, ironmonger of Deptford, issued this graphic token. The obverse refers to the battle of Hastings. The reverse recalls the disaster of the Royal George in Portsmouth Harbour in 1782. (DH Kent 13: 27 mm.)

1794 halfpenny. A Badminton private token issued to record the efforts of the Duke of Beaufort to alleviate a corn shortage. (DH Gloucestershire 31: 28 mm.)

1800 halfpenny. An Enniscorthy token commemorates the battle of Vinegar Hill, 1798. (DH Wexford 1-4: 28 mm.)

COMMEMORATING LOCAL EVENTS AND PERSONALITIES

1794 halfpenny. The imposing Shire Hall at Chelmsford, newly erected. (DH Essex 5: 28 mm.)

1795 halfpenny. Beccles displays its church and bridge. (DH Suffolk 16: 29 mm.)

1794 halfpenny. Bungay displays Bigod's Castle and on the reverse a plea 'For change not fraud'. (DH Suffolk 22: 28 mm.)

1793 halfpenny. Hawkins Bird, grocer of Bristol, shows Christ Church and on the reverse the East India House. (DH Somersetshire 89: 28 mm.)

1794 halfpenny. The fine display of the Botanic Gardens of Bath with biblical text. (DH Somersetshire 26: 29 mm.)

1797 penny. Dundee proudly displays its public building. (DH Angusshire 5: 31 mm.)

1796 halfpenny. A view of Montrose with a woman at a spinning wheel — a common piece of home furniture. (DH Angusshire 28: 28 mm.)

1796 halfpenny. A public building and shipping of Dundee. (DH Angusshire 16: 28 mm.)

1795 halfpenny. John Carter of Jermyn Street, London, shows a lady's shoe — catering to the fashion of the period. (DH Middlesex 275: 27 mm.)

1795 halfpenny. A striking display by Schooling and Son of Spitalfields, London, to illustrate their manufactures. (DH Middlesex 474: 27 mm.)

1795 halfpenny. The Boot and Shoe Manufactory of 1 Hatfield, Snow Hill, London. (DH Middlesex 323: 27 mm.)

1795 halfpenny. B. Guest, the issuer, a boot and shoe manufacturer of Blackfriars, London, shows examples of his wares. (DH Middlesex 308: 27 mm.)

1795 halfpenny. A filtering stone used for purifying water. A gallon (4.5 litres) took about an hour. (DH Middlesex 293: 27 mm.)

1794 halfpenny. Francis Shackleton of London, the issuer, illustrates the method of candlemaking. He was tallow maker to the Duke of York. (DH Middlesex 477: 28 mm.)

1795 halfpenny. Edward Neeton of St Marylebone, London, offers 'Wine, rum and brandy'. (DH Middlesex 390: 28 mm.)

Circa 1795 halfpenny. The Curriers' coat of arms is displayed. Reverse: a plough with the inscription 'God speed the plough' and 'Payable in Rupert Street St James's'. (DH Middlesex 472: 27 mm.)

1795 halfpenny. William Stinton of St James's Street, London, has a grasshopper to accompany his 'Fine teas of the rough flavour'. (DH Middlesex 904: 28 mm.)

1794 halfpenny. Fowler's token of whale fishery. (DH Middlesex 306: 28 mm.)

Circa 1795 halfpenny. Philip Deck, bookseller and postmaster of Bury, inscribes his initials PD above a crown. (DH Suffolk 26: 28 mm.)

Circa 1794 halfpenny. Rackham's Circulating Library of Bury. (DH Suffolk 29: 28 mm.)

1794 halfpenny. Conder's drapery warehouse. (DH Suffolk 35: 28 mm.)

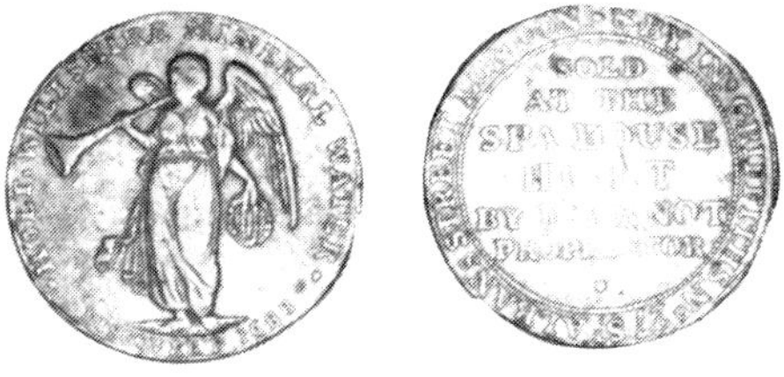

Circa 1795 halfpenny. The Spa House at Holt proclaims its mineral waters. (DH Wiltshire 3: 28 mm.)

1796 halfpenny. Sharpes, the grocers of Salisbury, advertise their 'Fine teas' with a view of the 'Cathedral church of Sarum'. (DH Wiltshire 21: 29 mm.)

1793 halfpenny. Huddersfield grocer John Downings displays the 'East India House.' (DH Yorkshire 15: 27 mm.)

1794 halfpenny. Talbort Fyan, grocer, shows a sugar loaf and a brandy bottle as part of his wares. (DH Dublin 308: 28 mm.)

1793 halfpenny. R. Campin, haberdasher of Norwich, displays a stocking, glove and knife and fork. (DH Norfolk 20: 28 mm.)

1796 halfpenny. Dunham and Yallop, goldsmiths of Norwich, show their fine shop front. (DH Norfolk 33: 28 mm.)

1793 halfpenny. Fieldings, grocers of Manchester, display the East India Company's bale mark. (DH Lancashire 130: 28 mm.)

1794 farthing. M. Lambe and Son, grocers of Bath, show a public building in Stall Street. (DH Somersetshire 111: 23 mm.)

1795 halfpenny. Niblock and Hunter's of Bristol, enterprising auctioneers, advertise their trade. (DH Somersetshire 100-101: 28 mm.)

1795 halfpenny. Bungay token 'For the use of trade.' (DH Suffolk 21: 28 mm.)

1812 penny. Thomas Birkinshaw, pawnbroker of Doncaster, issued this token with a figure of Justice. (D Yorkshire 80: 33 mm.)

Circa 1794 halfpenny. Spence's 'Glorious Plan'. (DH Middlesex 676: 28 mm.)

1796 halfpenny. Spence: contrast with a 'French republican'. (DH Middlesex 521: 27 mm.)

1796 halfpenny. Spence: 'A Marine Society boy'. Reverse: the turnstile neatly illustrates his address. (DH Middlesex 784: 28 mm.)

1795 halfpenny. Spence: 'Oddfellows.' Reverse: 'Tree of liberty'. (DH Middlesex 797: 28 mm.)

Circa 1795 halfpenny. Spence: a biting commentary on the harsh treatment of discharged sailors. (DH Middlesex 1048: 27 mm.)

Circa 1794 farthing. Spence: 'Advocates for the rights of man'. (DH Middlesex 1112: 20 mm.)

Circa 1794 halfpenny. Spence: Pitt and Fox 'Oddfellows'. Reverse: heart in hand. (DH Middlesex 804: 25 mm.)

1794 halfpenny. Spence: commentary on the famous free speech trials. (DH Middlesex 1012: 28 mm.)

1794 halfpenny. Spence: 'T. Hardy. Tried for high treason'. (DH Middlesex 1024: 27 mm.)

1794 halfpenny. Spence: commentary on French republicanism. (DH Middlesex 1016: 28 mm.)

1794 halfpenny. Spence: the trial of J. H. Tooke. (DH Middlesex 1046: 28 mm.)

1793 halfpenny. Token of the anti-Paine faction. (DH Middlesex 833: 29 mm.)

1795 halfpenny. The dreaded Newgate prison. Reverse: 'The residence' of four of the inmates. (DH Middlesex 396: 28 mm.)

1793 halfpenny. John Rooks of Norwich shows a mounted dragoon and a view of the barracks on the reverse. (DH Norfolk 46: 28 mm.)

1794 halfpenny. The Loyal Suffolk Yeomanry from Blything. (DH Suffolk 19: 29 mm.)

1797 twopence. The famous Cartwheel official copper coinage, issued in 1797 to alleviate the chronic coin shortage. (40 mm.)

1812 penny. The British Copper Company's rolling mills at Walthamstow. (D Essex 4-16: 34 mm.)

1813 penny. The Tees Bridge at Stockton. (D Durham 6: 34 mm.)

1811 penny. Crown Copper Company of Birmingham and Neath. (D Warwickshire 49: 35 mm.)

1811 penny. Bristol Brass and Copper Company. (D Somersetshire 81-87: 28 mm.)

Circa 1812 twopence. 'For change not profit'. Reverse: a shuttle of the cotton and bombazine manufacturer Robert Blake. (D Norfolk 17: 40 mm.)

1811 penny. A coal staith of the Bewick Main Colliery at Newcastle upon Tyne. (D Northumberland 16: 33 mm.)

1813 penny. A bale of cotton from the cotton works, Newcastle-under-Lyme. (D Staffordshire 89: 35 mm.)

1811 penny. A coal staith of the Bewick Main Colliery at Newcastle upon Tyne. (D

1812 halfpenny. The Roscoe Mill at Sheffield. (D Yorkshire 151: 28 mm.)

1813 penny. The Phoenix ironworks, Glasgow. (D Lanarkshire 1-5: 33 mm.)

1812 penny. The Picard leadworks at Hull. (D Yorkshire 87: 33 mm.)

1812 penny. Hobson's button works at Sheffield. (D Yorkshire 137: 34 mm.)

1812 penny. The Union Copper Company, Birmingham, shows hands clenched in common purpose. (D Warwickshire 65: 35 mm.)

1812 penny. The Birmingham and South Wales Company was a bogus concern used as cover for the sale of counterfeit tokens. (D Warwickshire 86: 35 mm.)

1811 penny. Rose Copper Company. (D Warwickshire 92-7: 35 mm.)

1811 penny. The 'Nail and Trace Manufactory' of Lye. (D Worcestershire 9: 33 mm.)

PLACES TO VISIT

The major museums housing collections of tokens are:

Ashmolean Museum, Beaumont Street, Oxford. Telephone: Oxford (0865) 512651.

Brighton Museum and Art Gallery, Church Street, Brighton. Telephone: Brighton (0273) 63005.

British Museum (Department of Coins), Great Russell Street, London WC1. Telephone: 01-636 1555.

Science Museum, Exhibition Road, South Kensington, London SW7. Telephone: 01-589 3456. Collection of industrial revolution tokens donated by the author.

It is advisable to enquire first when viewing is allowed. There are also numerous local museums throughout Britain where tokens can be seen. A visit to the National Museum of Labour History, Limehouse Town Hall, Commercial Road, London E14 (telephone: 01-515 3229), is particularly rewarding. Besides a fine token collection it houses a unique repository of historical documents of the Labour movement.

COLLECTING

Starting to collect tokens can develop into a pursuit of lifelong interest and pleasure. The possession of these objects of a past age is a stimulus to the acquiring of further knowledge about their remarkable history. It is advisable to proceed cautiously in buying the tokens that interest you. Poor quality specimens, unless of rare value, are best discarded in favour of those in better condition. You will soon become familiar with the various grades such as F (fine), VF (very fine), EF (extremely fine) and others; these distinctions reflect the sharp diversity of prices charged.

Tokens are bought from dealers, antique shops, market stalls, auction rooms and from press advertisements. *Coins and Medals* (monthly), *Coin* (fortnightly) and *Exchange and Mart* (weekly) are recognised channels. It is helpful to join your local numismatic society, where other token enthusiasts can be met. You will learn very soon about current market values, also the need to concentrate on acquiring only those pieces which are of importance to you.

FURTHER READING

Atkins, James. *The Tradesmen's Tokens of the Eighteenth Century.* W. S. Lincoln and Son, 1892.

Bell, R. C. *Commercial Coins, 1787-1804* (1963). *Tradesmen's Tickets and Private Tokens, 1785-1819* (1966). *Specious Tokens and Those Struck for General Circulation, 1784-1804* (1968). *Copper Commercial Coins, 1811-1819* (1964). All published by Corbitt and Hunter.

Berry, G. *Discovering Trade Tokens.* Shire Publications, 1969.

Dalton, R. and Hamer, S. H. *Provincial Token-Coinage of the Eighteenth Century* (1910). Seaby, reprinted 1969.

Davis, W. J. *Nineteenth-Century Token Coinage* (1906). Seaby, reprinted 1969.

Mathias, P. *English Trade Tokens: The Industrial Revolution Illustrated.* Abelard Schuman, 1962.

Waters, A. W. *Notes on Eighteenth-Century Tokens* (1954). *Notes on the Silver Tokens of the Nineteenth Century* (1957). Both published by Seaby.

Whiting, J. R. S. *Trade Tokens: A Social and Economic History.* David and Charles, 1971.

Williams, J. A. *Cornish Tokens.* Bradford Barton, 1971.

ACKNOWLEDGEMENTS

I would like to thank Pippa Richardson of the Science Museum for her valued assistance in reading the script and for her helpful comments. All illustrations are Crown Copyright, courtesy of the Science Museum. I also acknowledge the aid of the *History Workshop Journal,* in which an earlier version on this subject first appeared.